The Mysterious Strangers Within Us

By Peter Blackton

Illustrated by Donald E. Schlegel

cpi

contemporary perspectives, inc.

This book is distributed by Silver Burdett Company, Morristown,
New Jersey 07960.

Library of Congress Number: 79-17191

Art and Photo Credits
Cover illustration, Donald E. Schlegel
Photo on page 9, Culver Pictures, Inc.
Every effort has been made to trace the ownership of all
copyrighted material in this book and to obtain permission for its
use.

Library of Congress Cataloging in Publication Data

Blackton, Peter, 1922-
  The mysterious strangers within us.

  SUMMARY: Examines cases in which individuals have,
often without knowing it, displayed one or more
personalities.
  1. Multiple personality — Case studies — Juvenile
literature. [1. Multiple personality. 2. Mental illness] I.
Title.
RC569.5.M8B55   616.8'523   79-17191
ISBN 0-89547-083-7

Manufactured in the United States of America
ISBN 0-89547-083-7

Contents

Chapter 1

A Puzzling Conversation

It was a dark, wet night in the London of 1886. A thick fog wrapped the silent city. The only sounds heard were the footsteps of policemen. When they passed, the silence returned.

Suddenly, two angry voices broke the quiet. The shouting came from behind the locked door of a large, well-kept house.

A very rough, unpleasant voice spoke first. "You're nothing but a fool, Henry, a do-gooder! You waste your life caring for the sick and do nothing for yourself! You make me laugh!"

A gentle, more pleasant voice answered. "Edward, you are an evil and terrible man!"

"Evil and terrible?" the first voice cackled. "Why? Because I enjoy a life of pleasure? Because I destroy anyone who stands in my way? Henry, you're a soft-hearted fool!"

Now the gentle voice was raised to a shout.

"Edward, I want you out of this house — now!"

A snarl came from someplace deep inside Edward. He sounded like a wild animal. Then he screamed back at Henry.

"You want to get rid of *me*? I'm going to be with you for the rest of your life. We'll never be apart. NEVER!"

Had you opened the door to that house, you would have had quite a surprise. You would have found yourself in the office of a quiet and gentle medical doctor. But looking for the man with whom the doctor was arguing would have been a waste of time. The doctor was alone.

Had the good doctor done away with the evil man he called Edward? One look at this kind, good man would tell you the answer. Even in anger, this man could do no one any harm.

How is this possible? You've just heard *two* men arguing, their angry voices breaking the quiet of the

Dr. Henry Jekyll, at work in his laboratory. ▶

night. Yet now that you are inside the house you can see only one man.

The answer to this question is quite astonishing. Although Edward and Henry have very different personalities, *they share the same body.* Both voices were coming from the same man!

Robert Louis Stevenson made up these characters in his world-famous book, *Dr. Jekyll and Mr. Hyde.* It is a story that as a book, a play, and a motion picture has frightened people for a hundred years.

Because Henry Jekyll and Edward Hyde are so different, they hate each other. Jekyll is a gentle doctor, well liked by all. But Hyde is an evil, cunning monster. In Stevenson's story, whenever Dr. Jekyll drinks a chemical potion, he mysteriously becomes the dreadful Hyde.

Eventually, Dr. Jekyll cannot control Mr. Hyde, and he drinks the potion more and more often. Jekyll and Hyde battle for the one body they have between them. In the end Hyde wins.

Could such a thing happen in real life? Could the same body have more than one personality?

Since the time that Stevenson made up *Dr. Jekyll and Mr. Hyde,* doctors have uncovered many

The evil Mr. Hyde, as he appeared in the ▶
1932 movie *Dr. Jekyll and Mr. Hyde.*

mysterious but true cases of different "selves," or
personalities, that share the same body. There are
even cases of men and women whose bodies contain
more than two different personalities. The body of one
woman named Sybil Dorsett was shared by 16
different "selves."

Such people — Sybil Dorsett and others like her —
are said to have *multiple personalities*. These people
switch from one personality to another. Although they
exist within a single body, each self acts like a
completely different person.

For years, some of the finest scientists in the world
have studied cases of multiple personality. Yet in
most ways, these cases are as great a mystery today as
they ever were.

As early as 1890, doctors were trying to understand
why some people have multiple personalities. A small
part of what has been learned about them is what
follows in this book. If the stories of multiple
personalities seem frightening at first, remember one
thing. Modern doctors can help people with this
problem as never before because these cases are
now known. By studying them, doctors are learning
more and more about . . . *the mysterious strangers
within us.*

Chapter 2

A Long Sleep

Have you ever seen someone you think you know well change suddenly? Has a usually happy friend suddenly become very sad? You may even have said to him or her . . .

"I hardly know you. You seem like a different person. *You're not yourself today.*"

If you have seen this kind of change, imagine how a Pennsylvania farmer and his wife felt one morning in 1811 when their daughter suddenly became a total stranger.

Eighteen-year-old Mary Reynolds was a quiet, hardworking girl. Little about life seemed to interest her. She kept to herself and was shy around people. Most of the time she kept busy doing one job after another around her family's farm.

One morning Mary slept later than anyone else in the house. It was long past dawn, and Mary had not yet come down for breakfast. Her family wanted to know what was wrong. But no matter how hard they tried, they could not awaken her.

Mary slept all through the day. When evening came, some ten hours later, her eyes opened at last. Her family was happy to see the girl wake up. But their happiness did not last long. While the girl before them certainly looked like Mary, there was something very wrong with the voice they heard speaking to them. Eighteen-year-old Mary Reynolds sounded just like a baby!

Mary did not know one member of her own family. She did not recognize her own bedroom. The whole house was strange and frightening to her. Mary Reynolds had become someone else. Her 18-year-old body had the mind of a young child.

It was quite a shock to Mary's parents. How had this happened? Had the young woman completely lost her mind? Or was it just her memory? Puzzled, the family tried to stay calm. They began to teach Mary how to speak, read, and write, just as they had when she was young. They hoped the mysterious stranger would become the old Mary again soon. But for now they had to live with the fact that Mary had another personality.

The new Mary was a very good student. She learned to read and write much more quickly than most young children. In the beginning her main problem was learning to write words from left to right on the pages. She wrote her letters from right to left. But after just a few weeks she was reading and writing as well as anyone in the family.

The Reynolds family was pleased at how quickly Mary learned. But they were very unhappy about something else. Mary did not believe that she was part of their family. She was always pleasant, but she seemed afraid to get too close to them.

Many other differences between the old Mary and this stranger puzzled the family. Mary had never been an active girl. When she wasn't working, she sat quietly and kept to herself. The stranger, however, was outgoing and cheerful. She never seemed to run out of energy.

Unlike Mary, the stranger loved nature. She enjoyed riding horses and would often go out with a favorite horse for an all-day ride through the forest. The old Mary would have been afraid to be alone in the woods. But the stranger was fearless. One day a huge bear blocked her path in the woods. Mary would not let her horse turn back or run away. Instead she shouted at the great beast. When the bear reared up

on its hind legs and snarled at her, she leaped off her horse and frightened the bear away with a stick.

There was no doubt about it. Although they lived in the same body, Mary Reynolds and this stranger were two completely different people. Mary's family wondered if they would ever see her old personality return.

One morning, about five weeks later, the stranger slept later than usual. Mrs. Reynolds tried to awaken her but could not. When the girl finally opened her eyes and began to speak, the family could not believe their ears. It was the old Mary. *Mary Reynolds had returned to her home and family!*

Once again, Mary was the quiet, simple girl she had been before. But surprisingly, she had no memory of the many weeks she had spent as the talkative, nature-loving stranger. She could not figure out what had happened in all the time that had passed since she had gone to sleep "the night before." She thought she had only overslept.

Within a few days the Reynoldses had no doubt that their shy and timid daughter was back. Weeks passed and everyone felt sure the stranger was gone forever. But they were wrong. Soon Mary switched back to her other personality again. For many years, both selves shared Mary's body.

When she was 35 years old, Mary Reynolds went to live with her nephew, a clergyman. Her own family was gone, and the farm was lost. She needed work, and her nephew asked her to look after his house. He knew she needed the job, but that did not stop him from worrying about what to do if Mary's other personality returned. As it turned out, he need not have worried at all. Soon Mary had a new, *third* personality. Her new self was a happy combination of both the old Mary and the stranger. And it was this third self that stayed with her most of the time.

The new personality was quiet — but not as quiet as Mary had been. She was friendly and talkative — but this personality was never as active as the stranger's had been. Mary's new self enjoyed nature, but she never disappeared into the woods for entire days. The third self was a little like the old Mary and a little like the stranger.

Mary, the stranger, and Mary's third self lived in the same body for the next 25 years. Then, at the age of 61, Mary suddenly died. Three different personalities had shared her body. Yet not one of them ever knew about the other two. And her family never knew which Mary would greet them when she woke up in the morning.

The mystery of Mary Reynolds and her "other selves" was probably the first case ever reported of a

multiple personality. There must have been other such people before the nineteenth century, but no scientist ever wrote about them or studied them. Then, as medical scientists began to treat diseases of the mind like any other illness, more cases of multiple personality became known.

Toward the end of the nineteenth century there was another mysterious yet true story of a multiple personality. It was just as puzzling as the Mary Reynolds case.

◄ Mary Reynolds had become a third personality — a combination of the first Mary and the "stranger" who used to take over her body.

Chapter 3

The Disappearance of Ansel Bourne

Young Ansel Bourne was a carpenter. He was good at his craft. But around 1880, Bourne became very ill. For a short time he lost his sight and hearing. Unable to go on as a carpenter, he became a preacher. Ansel, now the Reverend Bourne, soon became a popular man. Everyone in his little village of Greene, Rhode Island, thought highly of him.

Mysteriously, his health returned. His sight and his hearing returned too. Ansel Bourne was a happy man again. He loved his new work. People respected and admired him. That was why everyone was so shocked by what happened next.

In January 1887, Ansel Bourne suddenly disappeared. Without a word to anyone, he vanished

from the village of Greene. Very little could be learned about his last day in town. He had gone to his bank and taken out quite a lot of money from his savings. But there was nothing strange about this. Many of his friends knew he was buying some land close to town.

It was then learned that Bourne had taken a horsecar to Pawtucket, Rhode Island. No one knew why he had gone to Pawtucket. But that was the last anyone saw of Ansel Bourne for about eight weeks.

In the middle of March 1887, Bourne's nephew, Andrew Harris, received a strange note. It was from a doctor in Norristown, Pennsylvania. Harris could hardly believe what he was reading.

The Norristown doctor wrote that he was treating a man he believed was insane. The man, however, kept insisting that he only lost his memory for a while. He told the doctor his name was Ansel Bourne. He was from Rhode Island, and his nephew, Andrew Harris, would come to take him home. The doctor went on to write that he and everyone else in Norristown knew this man by another name. Could Andrew Harris shed any light on the situation?

Harris sent the doctor a telegram right away. Hold the man, wrote Harris. He might very well be Ansel Bourne. Harris took the next train to Norristown.

When Harris got to Norristown he found that the "crazy man" was indeed his Uncle Ansel. But how and why his uncle had come to Norristown he could not say. Ansel Bourne did not know the reason either. He had no memory of the past two months.

Harris learned that his uncle had opened a store in Norristown. People there knew him as Mr. A.J. Brown. But Ansel remembered nothing, and he refused to go anywhere near the store. Harris closed the store and took his bewildered uncle home.

Ansel's wife took him to see Dr. William James. The doctor was sure he could easily hypnotize Ansel. Perhaps Ansel would then remember what had happened to him. It took Dr. James almost no time to put Bourne into a deep trance. Half asleep, half awake, Ansel Bourne was able to remember. He began to talk. Finally, the doctor was able to put together the true story of what happened to Ansel Bourne during those "lost" eight weeks.

In February, a gentleman who called himself A.J. Brown inspected a small empty store in Norristown and said he would rent it. He went into business immediately, selling candy, fruit, and other small items. Mr. Brown did well. He worked hard, paid his bills on time, and seemed very honest. He lived in the back room of the little shop. When he traveled, it was only to Philadelphia. There he bought the items he sold in his Norristown shop.

Everyone in Norristown quickly learned that Mr. A.J. Brown was a solid citizen. He went to church on Sunday. He was even called upon by his new friends to preach a sermon. There was nothing very strange or mysterious about Mr. Brown. He was a fine citizen of Norristown and a good neighbor.

On March 14, Mr. Brown's life took a very strange turn. Some of his neighbors heard him screaming from the back of his candy shop. Was their neighbor ill? Was he being robbed? What could possibly be wrong?

The first people to arrive at the little store found Mr. Brown in a panic. The usually quiet man was babbling. He made no sense at all. He looked at his neighbors as though he had never seen them before. "What am I doing in this little store?" he wanted to know. "Where am I? Who are these people now crowding around me?"

"But this is *your* store. You live here, Mr. Brown...."

Ansel was very frightened and confused. "Why do you call me Brown?" he shouted at them. "That's not

my name! My name is Ansel Bourne! And I'm from Rhode Island . . . What place is this?"

His friends, now fearing for his mind, again tried to calm him down. But when they told him that he was in Norristown, Pennsylvania, the poor fellow almost fainted.

Brown's neighbors, now very worried, called a doctor. The doctor feared that Mr. Brown's mind had snapped.

Dr. James, hearing the story, asked Ansel Bourne to remember how he had gone from Rhode Island to Pennsylvania. In his trance, Bourne answered that he had first gone to Boston, Massachusetts. Then he went on through New York City and Newark, New Jersey to spend ten days in Philadelphia. From there he got to Norristown, Pennsylvania, where, as Mr. A.J. Brown, he opened a little store.

Dr. James listened carefully. He had heard stories like Bourne's before. There were people, he knew, who had more than one personality. When one of these personalities showed itself to people, the other personality lay in hiding. Each appeared, one at a time, while the others hid from the world — *and from each other!*

Why had this mysterious stranger — A.J. Brown — suddenly appeared in Ansel Bourne? Was his early illness really an illness of the mind? When he had gone blind and deaf was his mind trying to shut out the world around him? Did A.J. Brown appear so that he would not have to be Ansel Bourne any more? Was there something making Ansel Bourne so unhappy about himself that he *needed* to be someone else?

Dr. James did not know. But somehow he was sure that Ansel Bourne would never again be bothered by Mr. A.J. Brown. As far as anyone knows, that is just the way things did turn out.

But what was it like for Ansel Bourne from then on? Did he spend the rest of his life wondering about that mysterious stranger who might come back at any time?

◄ Ansel Bourne's illness left him deaf and blind for a time. Was Bourne's new personality a result of that illness?

Chapter 4

Eve's Story

In 1957, Dr. Corbett H. Thigpen told the world a story about three women he had been treating. He called two of the women Eve and the third Jane. The three acted very differently. The first Eve was quiet and shy. The second Eve was bold and outgoing — "the life of the party." Jane was more clearheaded than the others. She was friendly and enjoyed having fun, but she was hardworking and serious too. You might say that she was a bit like both Eves combined.

Millions of people read Dr. Thigpen's book, *The Three Faces of Eve.* It became so popular that a movie was made about these three women. What made the doctor's story so fascinating? All three women were one person!

The story started when a troubled woman named Evelyn White came to Dr. Thigpen's office. Her own family doctor had sent her to him. She was not ill in a way her own doctor could cure. Her body was healthy as far as he could tell. But the health of her mind was another story. He thought a psychiatrist like Dr. Thigpen might be able to help the woman.

Evelyn White, called Eve by most people, explained her problem to Dr. Thigpen. She had been hearing a "voice" in her mind, and she was afraid she was "going crazy." The doctor felt sorry for the shy, quiet woman and wanted to help. He tried to make Eve talk more about herself, but she was so nervous that they did not make much progress.

After a few visits, Dr. Thigpen decided that Eve was quite sane. He wanted her to know that and began telling her what he felt. Suddenly, he had the shock of his life. Eve fell into a trance. She was no longer awake, yet not quite asleep. When she began talking again, it was in a different voice.

"Hi there, Doc!" the woman said.

This was not the shy and quiet Eve talking. This was a loud woman whose eyes seemed to dance and sparkle as she talked. Her very smile seemed wicked. This woman was a *different* Eve.

Having met the second Eve, the doctor now knew whose voice the first Eve had heard in her mind. Dr. Thigpen also knew that these two personalities could never peacefully share one body. Eve One and Eve Two must surely hate each other. To help the first Eve, he would somehow have to get rid of the second Eve. But *how?*

When Dr. Thigpen put Eve White in a trance, Eve Black would emerge. ▶

Dr. Thigpen had what he thought was a simple plan. He would talk with the second Eve and try to get to know her well. Then perhaps he could make her leave forever. From now on, he would call this other "self" Eve Black. He would hypnotize Eve White and once she was in a trance, he would ask to speak with Eve Black. In a trance, Eve White's mind would not be able to keep Eve Black from speaking out.

The plan worked well for a while. In the trance, Eve Black would appear whenever Dr. Thigpen asked for her. When he wanted Eve White again, he would simply ask Eve Black to call for her. Between the two Eves the doctor was getting to know his patient very well. Soon, he could call upon either Eve without having to use hypnosis at all.

Happily, Eve White was starting to look and feel better. Talking made her feel better. She was far less upset about herself. Dr. Thigpen felt he was really getting someplace. But his hopes were soon broken by a great surprise. One day, as the doctor was talking to one of the Eves, he suddenly heard a new voice. It was not Eve Black, nor was it Eve White. A *third* person was talking to him from the body of Eve White. The stranger's name was Jane. She told Dr. Thigpen she had just been "born." She was finding her new life great fun!

Jane was a little bit like both Eves. Like Eve White she spoke in a soft voice. Like Eve Black she had a lot to say. She seemed much wiser than either of the Eves. Yet she knew very few facts for someone her age. For example, when asked if she knew the name George Washington, she said she did not. She told the doctor she had no idea what the weather in springtime was like. Jane was in many ways a newborn baby who looked and talked like a woman.

Dr. Thigpen had to change his plan. He now had to deal with three people. Again and again he went over what he had heard from the two Eves about the life of his patient. If he was going to help this woman he had to put together her story from childhood onward. With Jane's help, he tried to piece everything together.

At five years old, Eve White loved her parents the way most children do. She was a well-mannered girl, quiet, shy, and always nice to the people around her.

But there was another "Eve" living inside her body, even at this young age. This Eve was not a very good or pleasant little girl at all. This second Eve was Eve White's other self, Eve Black.

Eve's mother and father knew nothing about Eve Black. When Eve's mother was very strict or punished her, Eve Black did not like it one bit. And she certainly didn't like it when her parents brought home a newborn pair of twins!

Eve White was happy and excited when the twins arrived. But Eve Black bit their tiny feet. It seemed that Eve White never knew when the second Eve would take over her body. Eve Black would mysteriously show up, and Eve White seemed to go to sleep until her other "self" left.

Eve White seemed to know nothing about those times when she was Eve Black. She never knew what Eve Black had been up to and was surprised to be punished for things she did not remember doing.

Dr. Thigpen found something else very puzzling about his two Eves. While Eve White knew nothing about Eve Black, Eve Black told him a great deal about Eve White. The doctor learned that Eve Black had always hated Eve White. Even when they were small children she hated having to live so close to her.

When the shy and quiet Eve White grew up, she found a job and moved to another town. Before moving away, Eve had often been frightened by her mother's strict rules and harsh punishments. She was also afraid of some of her mother's strange superstitions. When she was especially frightened of something, Eve Black "visited" more often. This would cause more trouble and more punishment. But

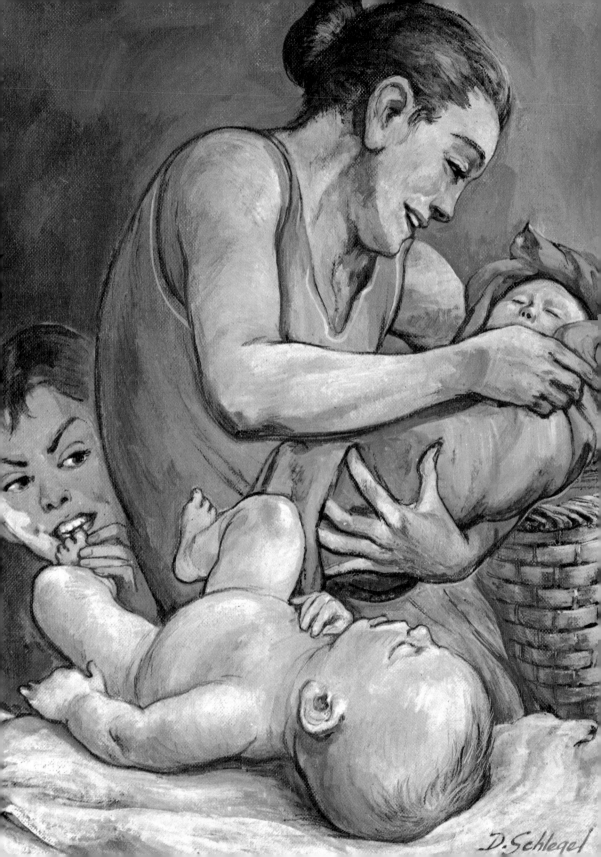

when she moved away from home, Eve Black stayed away for long periods of time. Eve White felt happier than she had ever felt before.

Eve met and married Ralph White. She stopped working and began raising a family.

Eve Black was not at all happy when Eve White got married. The second Eve wanted no part of having children or caring for them. She wanted to spend all her time at parties, restaurants, and theaters. Pleasure for herself was her only goal in life.

When the first Eve became the happy mother of a baby girl named Bonnie, the second Eve was even less happy. She was too "fun-loving" to sit around caring for some baby. She started to "visit" again.

Maybe it was the birth of Eve White's baby that brought Eve Black back. After all, when she was a child, the birth of the twins caused Eve Black to start a lot of trouble. Whatever it was, Eve Black started appearing much more often.

Ralph White, of course, had no way of knowing there was an Eve Black within the quiet and gentle woman he had married. As far as he knew, he was married to a woman with one personality. So when Eve White began to act like a completely different person, her husband Ralph was very confused.

One afternoon Ralph came home to find the baby all
alone. Eve was nowhere in sight. It just wasn't like
Eve to leave the baby this way. Something must be

wrong, he thought. Hours later the worried Ralph got the shock of his life. Eve came home dressed in very colorful "going-out" clothes he had never seen before. She was not at all worried about little Bonnie. What was more, she didn't know why he was so upset. She screamed at him and used language that he had never heard Eve use before. *Not herself*, he thought. *Not herself at all!*

Ralph did not know what to do. He decided that a vacation might do Eve some good. She had been working too hard, he thought. A little rest and she would be herself again. He would take care of the baby and the house himself. He asked Eve if she would like to visit a favorite cousin of hers who lived in a nearby town. His wife (Eve White? Eve Black?) liked the idea very much and she left on her vacation.

Eve's cousin was quite surprised at the change she saw in Eve. Suddenly Eve loved fancy clothes, expensive restaurants, shopping trips, and movies. This was not the quiet Eve her cousin remembered. She was puzzled and found herself hoping Eve would leave soon.

Eve Black, however, did not want to go home. She did not want Eve White's family life. She stayed on at her cousin's home.

Eve's cousin had no idea that this guest in her ▶
home was Eve White's other self — Eve Black.

Ralph White was becoming worried about his wife's being away so long. He telephoned Eve to find out why she was not home yet. Eve Black rudely told him she was having a fine time. She planned to make her vacation much longer. She had no idea when she would be back — or even if she would be back at all.

Now Ralph was more than upset. He was quite angry. He got into his car and drove the 50 miles to where Eve was staying. He asked his wife to go home with him. But the trip had been a waste of time. He was dealing with an angry Eve Black. She told Ralph she would never come home again.

The unhappy Ralph drove back home that same night. Sleep was impossible. He sat down to think the whole terrible thing through. He had been doing just that for about two hours when he suddenly heard a key in the front door. The door opened and there stood a smiling Eve. She ran to the stunned man, threw her arms around him, and told him how happy she was to be home.

Life went on this way for Ralph and Eve. When Eve White was in control, everything was wonderful. When Eve Black took over, life was a bad dream. Eve White never seemed to remember the awful moments when she was Eve Black.

That was when their family doctor suggested they meet with Dr. Thigpen. Eve White seemed to be a sane woman who had a terrible problem and didn't even know it. If she were to *stay* sane, she would need help — *now!*

Dr. Corbett Thigpen thought about Eve's story from the time she was a child. He knew so much about the two Eves, and yet he felt he knew so little. Now, sitting in his office was a third "Eve" — someone called Jane — who told him *she had just been born!*

Jane was the fastest learner Dr. Thigpen had ever met. She was stronger than both Eves, and yet she was much more even-tempered. She was so bright and so fine a person that the doctor decided she could be very helpful.

Jane seemed to help Eve White keep Eve Black from "visiting" as often as she had. Over the years, as Eve Black stopped coming around as much, Jane also "visited" less often.

Mysteriously, Eve White became less and less quiet and shy. She was happier than ever and for much longer periods of time. The world was becoming a far more beautiful place for her.

Dr. Thigpen never gave up on Eve. He watched her become Eve White again, a much happier person than she had been when she started visiting him years earlier.

Perhaps the best part, for both doctor and patient, was that there finally seemed to be real hope. Eve, a woman with three different personalities, was finally becoming *one* person for the first time in her life.

A Final Word

Since the time of Mary Reynolds — almost 170 years ago — many cases of multiple personalities have been studied by scientists and doctors. Today we know a good deal more about the problem. Yet a lot more work remains to be done.

Unlike Robert Louis Stevenson's character, Mr. Hyde, a person's second self does not have to be cruel or vicious. Both of Ansel Bourne's personalities, for example, were very likeable. And although Eve Black was selfish, she was not all that different from some quite normal people.

It is very important to understand that people with multiple personalities are *not* taken over by someone

or something outside their bodies. No demon or devil has suddenly decided to invade their minds in search of a home.

Doctors have found that the problem lies within the people themselves. It is not yet clear exactly what goes wrong or how it can be prevented. But as doctors study more and more cases, the answer will be found.

Then perhaps those mysterious strangers within us will disappear forever.